Beyond The Walls: Unlocking Courage to Defeat Claustrophobia

By
Trevor Johnson

Introduction

Did you know that claustrophobia affects approximately 5-7% of the global population? That means that millions of people around the world struggle with the fear of confined spaces every day. But there is hope.

In this book, we will explore the strategies and techniques that can help you overcome claustrophobia and unlock the courage within you to face your fears head-on.

Claustrophobia, a type of anxiety disorder, is characterized by an intense fear of closed-in spaces. The symptoms can range from mild discomfort to full-blown panic attacks, making it difficult for those affected to navigate everyday situations. However, with the right tools and support, you can learn to manage and conquer your claustrophobia.

From recognizing triggers and managing panic attacks to breathing techniques and gradual exposure therapy, we will delve into a variety of methods that can help you regain control over your fear. We will also explore the importance of rewiring negative thought patterns through cognitive-behavioral therapy and creating safe spaces that promote comfort and relaxation.

So, if you're ready to break free from the constraints of claustrophobia and live a life beyond the walls, let's dive in and discover the keys to unlocking your courage.

Understanding Claustrophobia: Causes and Symptoms

If you've ever felt your heart race and your palms sweat in small spaces, you're not alone - claustrophobia can strike anyone, and understanding its causes and symptoms is the first step towards overcoming it.

Claustrophobia is an anxiety disorder characterized by an intense fear of confined spaces. The causes of claustrophobia can vary from person to person, but it is often linked to traumatic experiences, such as being trapped in an elevator or experiencing a panic attack in a small room. Additionally, some individuals may develop claustrophobia due to a genetic predisposition or a chemical imbalance in the brain.

The symptoms of claustrophobia can be both physical and psychological. Physical symptoms may include rapid heartbeat, shortness of breath, sweating, trembling, and feeling lightheaded or dizzy. Psychological symptoms may include intense fear, a sense of impending doom, and a strong desire to escape or avoid confined spaces. These symptoms can be debilitating and may interfere with daily life and activities.

Fortunately, there are management techniques that can help individuals cope with and overcome claustrophobia. One common technique is exposure therapy, where individuals gradually expose themselves to small spaces in a controlled and safe environment, allowing them to become desensitized to their fears. Breathing exercises and relaxation techniques can also be helpful in reducing anxiety symptoms. Cognitive-behavioral therapy (CBT) is another effective approach that focuses on identifying and challenging negative thoughts and beliefs associated with confined spaces.

Understanding the causes and symptoms of claustrophobia is crucial in overcoming this anxiety disorder. By implementing management techniques and seeking professional help, individuals can learn to unlock their courage and defeat claustrophobia, allowing them to live a life free from the limitations of their fears.

Recognizing Triggers and Managing Panic Attacks

To effectively manage panic attacks, you must first recognize the triggers and develop strategies to cope with them.

Panic attacks can be overwhelming, but by understanding what causes them and implementing techniques to manage them, you can regain control and overcome the fear that claustrophobia brings.

Identifying triggers is crucial in managing panic attacks. These triggers can vary from person to person, but common ones include enclosed spaces, crowded areas, elevators, and even certain sounds or smells. Being aware of these triggers allows you to anticipate and prepare for potential panic attacks. It's important to remember that triggers can change over time, so regularly reassessing your triggers is essential.

Once you have identified your triggers, it's time to develop strategies to cope with panic attacks. One effective technique is deep breathing. When you feel a panic attack coming on, focus on taking slow, deep breaths. This can help calm your body and reduce the intensity of the panic attack. Another strategy is visualization. Close your eyes and imagine yourself in a calm and open space. This can help shift your focus away from the triggering environment and alleviate anxiety.

Seeking support from loved ones or joining a support group can also be beneficial. Talking to others who understand what you're going through can provide comfort and encouragement. Additionally, consider consulting with a mental health professional who specializes in anxiety disorders. They can provide you with personalized strategies and techniques to manage panic attacks.

Remember, managing panic attacks takes time and practice. Be patient with yourself and celebrate small victories along the way. With determination and the right tools, you can conquer your claustrophobia and unlock the courage to live beyond the walls.

Breathing Techniques for Calming Anxiety

Deep breathing techniques can help alleviate anxiety and promote a sense of calmness during moments of high stress. When you find yourself feeling overwhelmed or anxious, taking a moment to focus on your breath can make a significant difference in how you feel.

Here are some breathing exercises and visualization techniques that can help you regain control and find peace within yourself:

- **Box breathing:** This technique involves inhaling for a count of four, holding the breath for a count of four, exhaling for a count of four, and holding the breath again for a count of four. Repeat this pattern several times, focusing on the rhythm of your breath. This exercise can help regulate your breathing and bring you back to a state of calm.
- **Diaphragmatic breathing:** Also known as belly breathing, this exercise involves inhaling deeply through your nose, allowing your belly to expand as you fill your lungs with air. Exhale slowly through your mouth, feeling your belly deflate. Repeat this process several times, focusing on the sensation of your breath moving in and out of your body. This technique can help relax your muscles and reduce tension.
- **Visualization techniques:** Combine deep breathing with visualizing a peaceful scene or a

place where you feel safe and calm. Close your eyes and imagine yourself in that environment, paying attention to the sights, sounds, and smells. As you inhale, imagine breathing in the tranquility of that place, and as you exhale, release any stress or tension you may be holding onto. This technique can transport you to a more serene state of mind.

Remember, practicing these breathing exercises and visualization techniques regularly can help you build resilience and better cope with anxiety. Take a few moments each day to connect with your breath and find peace within yourself.

Gradual Exposure Therapy: Facing Your Fears

Confronting your fears head-on through gradual exposure therapy can empower you to overcome anxiety and reclaim control over your life. Fear exposure, also known as desensitization therapy, is a highly effective method for treating claustrophobia.

By gradually exposing yourself to the situations that trigger your fear, you can learn to manage your anxiety and ultimately conquer it.

During gradual exposure therapy, you will work with a qualified therapist who will guide you through a series of carefully planned steps. The process begins with identifying your specific triggers and creating a fear hierarchy. This hierarchy is a list of situations that provoke anxiety, ranked from least to most distressing.

Starting with the least distressing situation, you will gradually expose yourself to each fear-inducing scenario, allowing yourself to become more comfortable and less anxious over time.

The goal of gradual exposure therapy is to desensitize yourself to the situations that trigger your claustrophobia. By facing your fears in a controlled and supportive environment, you can break the cycle of anxiety and avoidance. Each time you confront a fear-inducing situation, you will learn that you can tolerate the discomfort and that your anxiety will eventually subside.

It's important to remember that gradual exposure therapy is a gradual process. It's normal to feel anxious and uncomfortable at first, but with time and practice, you will build resilience and confidence. Your therapist will be there to support and guide you throughout the journey, providing reassurance and teaching you coping strategies to manage your anxiety.

By embracing gradual exposure therapy and facing your fears, you can unlock the courage within you to defeat claustrophobia. You have the power to take control of your life and overcome the limitations that anxiety has placed upon you. With each step forward, you will become stronger and more resilient, reclaiming your freedom and living life to the fullest.

Cognitive-Behavioral Therapy: Rewiring Negative Thought Patterns

Imagine rewiring the negative thought patterns that hold you back and replacing them with empowering beliefs through cognitive-behavioral therapy. This form of therapy is a powerful tool in helping individuals overcome claustrophobia by challenging irrational beliefs and changing the way they think about confined spaces.

Here are four ways cognitive-behavioral therapy can help you unlock courage and defeat claustrophobia:

- **Recognizing negative thought patterns:** Through therapy, you'll learn to identify the negative thoughts that contribute to your fear of confined spaces. By becoming aware of these patterns, you can begin to challenge and replace them with more positive and rational beliefs.
- **Challenging irrational beliefs:** Cognitive-behavioral therapy will guide you in questioning the validity of your fears. You'll examine the evidence supporting your negative beliefs and work to replace them with more realistic and helpful thoughts. This process allows you to break free from the cycle of fear and anxiety.
- **Developing coping strategies:** With the help of a therapist, you'll learn practical techniques to

manage your anxiety when faced with confined spaces. These strategies may include deep breathing exercises, visualization, or progressive muscle relaxation, among others. By practicing these coping mechanisms, you'll gain confidence in your ability to handle challenging situations.

- **Gradual exposure to triggers:** Cognitive-behavioral therapy often involves gradually exposing yourself to the situations or environments that trigger your claustrophobia. This exposure allows you to confront your fears in a controlled and supportive environment, helping you build resilience and decrease your anxiety over time.

Cognitive-behavioral therapy offers a transformative approach to overcoming claustrophobia. By rewiring negative thought patterns and challenging irrational beliefs, you can unlock the courage within you to face confined spaces with confidence and resilience. Remember, with the right support and guidance, you have the power to defeat claustrophobia and live a life free from fear.

Seeking Professional Help: Therapy and Medication Options

If you're struggling with claustrophobia, it's essential to seek professional help through therapy and medication options. Finding relief and managing your symptoms effectively can be achieved through these methods.

When it comes to medication, there are several options available that can help alleviate the symptoms of claustrophobia. Healthcare professionals may prescribe medications such as selective serotonin reuptake inhibitors (SSRIs) or benzodiazepines to reduce anxiety and panic associated with claustrophobic situations. It's important to note that medication effectiveness can vary from person to person, so finding the right medication and dosage may require some trial and error.

In addition to medication, alternative therapies can also be beneficial in treating claustrophobia. These therapies can complement traditional treatment methods and include techniques like mindfulness meditation, relaxation exercises, and exposure therapy. Mindfulness meditation helps develop a greater sense of awareness and control over thoughts, while relaxation exercises reduce anxiety and promote a sense of calm. Exposure therapy involves gradually exposing oneself to confined spaces in a controlled and safe manner, allowing the individual to confront and overcome their fears over time.

Seeking professional help is not a sign of weakness, but rather a courageous step towards taking control of your claustrophobia. A trained therapist can provide you with the necessary tools and techniques to cope with your symptoms and overcome the challenges associated with this condition. They can also work with you to find the most suitable medication and dosage to effectively manage your symptoms. Remember, you don't have to face claustrophobia alone, and professional help is available to support you on your journey to finding relief and reclaiming your life.

Support Groups and Peer Counseling

Joining a support group or seeking out peer counseling can provide you with a sense of connection and understanding as you navigate the challenges of managing your claustrophobia. Knowing that you're not alone in your struggles can be a great source of comfort and encouragement. Peer support can offer valuable insights and coping strategies from individuals who have firsthand experience with claustrophobia.

Here are three ways in which support groups and peer counseling can benefit you:

- **Emotional Support:** Connecting with others who share similar experiences can help alleviate feelings of isolation and provide a safe space to express your emotions. Support groups offer a supportive and non-judgmental environment where you can openly discuss your fears and anxieties related to claustrophobia. Sharing your thoughts and hearing others' stories can help you gain perspective, reduce stress, and build resilience.
- **Practical Advice:** Support groups and peer counseling can provide practical advice and tips for managing claustrophobia in everyday situations. Members may share techniques they've found effective, such as deep breathing exercises or visualization techniques. Learning

from others who've successfully overcome their fears can inspire you to try new coping mechanisms and find what works best for you.

- **Online Forums:** In addition to in-person support groups, there are also online forums and communities dedicated to claustrophobia. These platforms offer a convenient way to connect with others who understand what you're going through. You can share your experiences, ask questions, and receive support from people all over the world. Online forums provide a sense of anonymity, making it easier for some individuals to open up and seek guidance.

Remember, joining a support group or seeking peer counseling is a personal choice. It's important to find a group or community that aligns with your needs and values. With the support of others who've faced similar challenges, you can gain the courage to overcome your claustrophobia and live a more fulfilling life.

Mindfulness and Meditation for Relaxation

Practicing mindfulness and meditation can help you find peace and calmness amidst the challenges of managing claustrophobia. When faced with situations that trigger your claustrophobia, such as being in enclosed spaces or crowded rooms, mindfulness techniques and meditation practices can provide you with effective tools to cope and overcome your fears.

Mindfulness involves focusing your attention on the present moment, paying attention to your thoughts and feelings without judgment. By practicing mindfulness, you can learn to observe your claustrophobic thoughts and physical sensations without getting caught up in them. This allows you to create a sense of distance between yourself and your claustrophobia, reducing its power over you.

Meditation is another valuable practice for managing claustrophobia. By engaging in meditation, you can cultivate a state of deep relaxation and inner peace. Through various meditation techniques, such as deep breathing exercises or guided imagery, you can learn to redirect your thoughts away from your claustrophobia and towards a state of calmness and tranquility.

In addition to helping you relax, mindfulness and meditation can also enhance your overall well-being. They've been shown to reduce stress, anxiety, and depression, which are often associated with claustrophobia. By incorporating mindfulness and meditation into your daily routine, you can improve your mental and emotional resilience, making it easier to face and overcome your claustrophobic triggers.

It's important to remember that mindfulness and meditation are skills that require practice and patience. You may find it helpful to seek guidance from a trained professional or join a meditation group to learn different techniques and receive support from others who are also managing claustrophobia. With consistent effort and a compassionate attitude towards yourself, you can unlock the courage to defeat claustrophobia and live a life beyond the walls of fear.

Creating a Safe Space: Designing Comfortable Environments

Create a sanctuary for yourself by designing comfortable environments that provide a sense of calm and security, helping you find solace in spaces free from the grip of claustrophobia.

When it comes to creating a safe space, there are design principles and ergonomic furniture that can greatly contribute to your overall comfort and well-being.

Here are four key elements to consider when designing a comfortable environment:

- **Openness**: Opt for open floor plans that create a sense of spaciousness. Avoid clutter and embrace minimalism to reduce visual distractions. By allowing natural light to flow freely and using light, neutral colors, you can create a calming atmosphere that promotes relaxation.
- **Proper Lighting**: Lighting plays a crucial role in the overall ambiance of a space. Incorporate a mix of natural and artificial lighting to create a balanced and soothing environment. Soft, warm lights can help create a cozy atmosphere, while adjustable lighting options allow you to customize the brightness based on your preferences.
- **Ergonomic Furniture**: Invest in ergonomic furniture that supports your body and promotes

good posture. Adjustable chairs, standing desks, and supportive mattresses can alleviate physical discomfort and contribute to a more relaxed state of mind. Consider using soft, plush textures for upholstery to evoke a sense of comfort and coziness.

- **Nature-Inspired Elements**: Incorporate nature-inspired elements, such as indoor plants and natural materials, to create a connection with the outdoors. Plants not only add a touch of greenery but also improve air quality and create a calming effect. Natural materials like wood and stone can add warmth and a sense of grounding to the space.

By implementing these design principles and incorporating ergonomic furniture, you can create a safe and comfortable environment that supports you in overcoming claustrophobia. Remember, your sanctuary should be a reflection of your personal style and preferences, providing you with a space where you can truly unwind and find peace.

Self-Help Strategies for Coping with Claustrophobia

Embracing a mindset of expansion and freedom, finding ways to breathe and navigate through tight spaces can be like discovering hidden passageways in the labyrinth of claustrophobia. When faced with the overwhelming fear and anxiety that claustrophobia can bring, it's crucial to equip yourself with self-help strategies that can provide relief and a sense of control.

Two effective techniques to consider are breathing exercises and visualization techniques.

Deep breathing exercises are a powerful tool to help calm the mind and relax the body. By focusing on your breath and consciously taking slow, deep breaths, you can activate the body's relaxation response and reduce feelings of panic.

Practice diaphragmatic breathing by inhaling deeply through your nose, allowing your abdomen to expand, and then exhaling slowly through your mouth. Repeat this process several times, allowing yourself to feel more grounded and centered in the present moment.

Visualization techniques can also be beneficial in coping with claustrophobia. Close your eyes and imagine yourself in a peaceful and open space, such as a beautiful garden or a spacious beach.

Engage all your senses and try to immerse yourself fully in this imaginary environment.

Visualize the sensation of fresh air on your skin, the sound of birds chirping, or the feeling of sand beneath your feet. This technique can help shift your focus away from the confined space you may be in, allowing you to feel a sense of expansiveness and freedom.

Remember, overcoming claustrophobia is a journey that requires patience and perseverance. By incorporating breathing exercises and visualization techniques into your self-help arsenal, you can empower yourself to face tight spaces with courage and resilience. Be kind to yourself throughout this process and celebrate each small victory along the way.

Overcoming Claustrophobia in Everyday Situations

Conquer the challenge of claustrophobia by discovering a newfound sense of freedom in everyday situations. Overcoming fears isn't an easy task, but with the right coping strategies, you can regain control and live a more fulfilling life.

Claustrophobia, the fear of enclosed spaces, can be debilitating and restrict your daily activities. However, by implementing a few techniques, you can gradually overcome this fear and navigate through everyday situations with confidence.

One effective strategy is deep breathing. When faced with a triggering situation, take slow, deep breaths to calm your mind and body. This simple technique helps reduce anxiety and allows you to think more clearly.

Another helpful method is visualization. Picture yourself in a relaxing and open space, visualizing the feeling of freedom and safety. This mental exercise can help alleviate the anxiety associated with enclosed spaces.

Additionally, it's crucial to challenge your negative thoughts. Remind yourself that fear is just an emotion and doesn't define you. Replace negative thoughts with positive affirmations, such as "I'm in control" or "I can handle this situation." By reframing your mindset, you can build resilience and face your fears head-on.

Gradual exposure to enclosed spaces is another effective way to overcome claustrophobia. Start with small, manageable situations and gradually increase the intensity. For example, begin by spending a few minutes in a slightly confined space, gradually progressing to longer periods or more enclosed areas. This progressive exposure allows your brain to adapt and desensitize to the fear.

Remember, overcoming claustrophobia is a journey that requires patience and perseverance. Seek support from loved ones or consider joining a support group where you can connect with others facing similar challenges. With time and practice, you can unlock the courage within you to defeat claustrophobia and enjoy the freedom that lies beyond the walls.

Maintaining Long-Term Success: Self-Care and Relapse Prevention

Maintaining long-term success in overcoming claustrophobia requires consistent self-care and practicing relapse prevention, ensuring that you continue to embrace a life of freedom and confidence in everyday situations.

It's important to remember that overcoming claustrophobia is a journey, and even though you may have made significant progress, it's crucial to continue taking care of yourself and implementing strategies to prevent any setbacks. With the right self-care techniques and relapse prevention strategies, you can maintain your newfound freedom and live without the limitations of claustrophobia.

Self-care techniques play a vital role in maintaining long-term success. It's essential to prioritize your mental and emotional well-being. Engaging in relaxation exercises, such as deep breathing or meditation, can help you manage any anxiety or stress that may arise. Taking care of your physical health is equally important. Regular exercise, a balanced diet, and sufficient sleep can contribute to overall well-being, reducing the likelihood of experiencing claustrophobic symptoms.

In addition to self-care, practicing relapse prevention strategies is crucial. Identifying triggers that may lead to claustrophobic episodes is key. Once you have identified these triggers, you can develop coping mechanisms to navigate through challenging situations. This may include using visualization techniques, positive self-talk, or seeking support from a trusted friend or therapist. It's also helpful to create a plan for managing potential relapses, ensuring that you have strategies in place to address any setbacks that may occur.

Remember, maintaining long-term success in overcoming claustrophobia requires consistent effort and dedication. By prioritizing self-care and implementing relapse prevention strategies, you can continue to embrace a life of freedom and confidence, beyond the walls of claustrophobia.

Frequently Asked Questions

Can claustrophobia be cured completely?

Yes, claustrophobia can be effectively treated, although a complete cure may not be possible for everyone. Cognitive Behavioral Therapy (CBT) has shown to be highly effective in reducing the symptoms of claustrophobia. Through CBT, individuals can learn to challenge and change their negative thought patterns and behaviors associated with confined spaces.

Additionally, self-help techniques such as relaxation exercises and gradual exposure to confined spaces can also be beneficial in managing and overcoming claustrophobia.

Are there any alternative therapies or treatments for claustrophobia?

There are several alternative therapies and natural remedies that can be helpful in treating claustrophobia. Some people find relief through cognitive-behavioral therapy, which helps to change negative thought patterns and behaviors associated with claustrophobia.

Other options include exposure therapy, relaxation techniques, and using essential oils such as lavender or chamomile to promote a sense of calm.

It's important to find what works best for you and to consult with a healthcare professional for guidance.

How long does it usually take to see progress with gradual exposure therapy?

Seeing progress with gradual exposure therapy varies from person to person, but the journey is worth it. It's like a ray of sunlight breaking through the darkness, offering hope and liberation.

As you face your fears in a safe and controlled environment, you'll start to notice small victories along the way. Over time, the benefits of gradual exposure therapy become evident as you gain confidence, conquer your claustrophobia, and step into a world without limits.

What are some common misconceptions about cognitive-behavioral therapy for claustrophobia?

Misconceptions about cognitive-behavioral therapy (CBT) for claustrophobia are common. One misconception is that CBT is not effective in treating claustrophobia. However, numerous studies have shown the effectiveness of CBT in reducing claustrophobic symptoms and improving overall quality of life.

Another misconception is that CBT is a quick fix. While progress can vary for each individual, CBT is a gradual process that requires time and commitment. It is important to understand the effectiveness and commitment required for CBT to successfully treat claustrophobia.

Are there any specific medications that are commonly prescribed for claustrophobia?

When it comes to medication options for claustrophobia, there are a few commonly prescribed drugs. These can help alleviate symptoms and make you feel more comfortable in confined spaces. However, like with any medication, there are potential side effects to consider.

It's important to discuss your options with a healthcare professional who can guide you in finding the right medication for you. Remember, medication is just one tool in the toolbox for managing claustrophobia.

Conclusion

Congratulations! You've now reached the end of this article on overcoming claustrophobia. By understanding the causes and symptoms, recognizing triggers, and utilizing techniques such as breathing exercises and exposure therapy, you've taken the first steps towards conquering your fears.

Remember, it's important to rewire negative thought patterns and create a safe space for yourself. With self-help strategies and the courage to face your fears in everyday situations, you can continue to overcome claustrophobia.

Stay committed to self-care and relapse prevention, and you'll unlock the courage to thrive beyond the walls of your fears.

Key Takeaways

- Strategies and techniques, such as exposure therapy and breathing techniques, can help overcome claustrophobia.
- Cognitive-Behavioral Therapy (CBT) is effective in rewiring negative thought patterns and teaching practical coping strategies.
- Support from loved ones and mental health professionals is beneficial in managing and overcoming claustrophobia.
- Creating a comfortable environment with open floor plans, minimal clutter, proper lighting, ergonomic furniture, and nature-inspired elements promotes calmness and relaxation.